Views of Venice

NATIONAL GALLERY OF ART   a book of postcards

Pomegranate

SAN FRANCISCO

Pomegranate Communications, Inc.
Box 808022, Petaluma CA 94975
800 227 1428; www.pomegranate.com

Pomegranate Europe Ltd.
Unit 1, Heathcote Business Centre, Hurlbutt Road
Warwick, Warwickshire CV34 6TD, UK
[+44] 0 1926 430111; sales@pomeurope.co.uk

ISBN 978-0-7649-5843-4
Pomegranate Catalog No. AA671

Pomegranate publishes books of postcards on a wide range of subjects.
Please contact the publisher for more information.

Cover designed by Patrice Morris
Printed in Korea
20 19 18 17 16 15 14 13 12 11   10 9 8 7 6 5 4 3 2 1

To facilitate detachment of the postcards from this book, fold each card along its perforation line before tearing.

The stunning lagoon city of Venice has long attracted painters and printmakers seeking to capture her brilliant architecture and limpid light. Canaletto was the most renowned among the view painters of Venice in the eighteenth century, but other artists also were in great demand, including Canaletto's nephew Bernardo Bellotto, his rival Francesco Guardi, and his follower Antonio Joli. These and other painters satisfied the market for images that reminded visitors of their experience abroad after their return home.

While in Venice on the Grand Tour, travelers marveled at the religious, political, and social center of the city, the Basilica of San Marco and its adjacent piazza, one of the most striking architectural ensembles in Europe. Visitors also admired the Gothic and Renaissance palaces that lined the Grand Canal, the numerous opulent churches, and the famous Rialto Bridge. Tourists often brought back souvenirs, including sculptures, prints and drawings, books, and particularly view paintings of these familiar and storied sights.

After the fall of Venice to the French in 1797, foreign artists dominated the market in views of the former republic. Richard Parkes Bonington was among the British artists to represent Venice in the early nineteenth century, followed by the more prolific painter and watercolorist Joseph Mallord William Turner.

Turner, who visited Venice three times during his life, moved his attention away from the topographical focus of eighteenth-century view painters to the creation of dazzling effects of light and atmosphere. French writers and artists also discovered the charms of the picturesque city. Stendhal wrote admiringly of the city, perhaps providing the inspiration for the Venetian works of Jules-Romain Joyant, the self-styled "French Canaletto." Later, Claude Monet's only trip to Venice in 1908 produced important modernist works of major sites. Among other European artists, German painters deserve particular attention for capturing the spell of the enchanting city.

After the Civil War, Americans began to visit Venice, Rome, and Florence in large numbers. James McNeill Whistler and John Singer Sargent were among the most significant American artists to depict Venice in the later nineteenth century. In contrast to contemporary British and French painters, they sought to capture the local inhabitants' experience. Although Whistler and Sargent sometimes rendered the monumental and well-known attractions of the city, they also emphasized a Venice of the Venetians, depicting the narrow alleys, minor squares, and deserted canals that were an integral part of everyday life.

Views of Venice

Antonio Joli (Italian, c. 1700–1777)
Procession in the Courtyard of the Ducal Palace, Venice,
1742 or after

Oil on canvas, 160.7 x 221.6 cm
Gift of Mrs. Barbara Hutton 1945.15.1

707 782 9000   WWW.POMEGRANATE.COM

Pomegranate

Views of Venice

James McNeill Whistler (American, 1834–1903)
Nocturne, 1879/1880

Etching in brown, 20 x 29.5 cm
Rosenwald Collection 1943.3.8517

707 782 9000   WWW.POMEGRANATE.COM

Pomegranate

Views of Venice

William Stanley Haseltine (American, 1835–1900)
Shipping Along the Molo in Venice, unknown date

Watercolor and gouache over graphite
on brown paper, 31.2 x 47.8 cm
Gift of Helen Haseltine Plowden 1968.11.1

Views of Venice

Antonio Joli (Italian, c. 1700–1777)
*Procession of Gondolas in the Bacino
di San Marco, Venice*, 1742 or after

Oil on canvas, 160.7 x 221.6 cm
Gift of Mrs. Barbara Hutton 1945.15.2

707 782 9000   WWW.POMEGRANATE.COM

Pomegranate

Views of Venice

Canaletto (Italian, 1697–1768)
The Maundy Thursday Festival Before
the Ducal Palace in Venice, c. 1765

Pen and brown ink with gray wash, heightened
with white gouache, over black chalk on laid paper
Wolfgang Ratjen Collection, Paul Mellon Fund 2007.111.55

Views of Venice

Bernardo Bellotto (Italian, 1722–1780)
The Campo di SS. Giovanni e Paolo, Venice, 1743/1747

Oil on canvas, 70.8 x 111 cm
Widener Collection 1942.9.7

Views of Venice

John Singer Sargent (American, 1856–1925)
Street in Venice, 1882

Oil on wood, 45.1 x 53.9 cm
Gift of the Avalon Foundation 1962.4.1

WWW.POMEGRANATE.COM

707 782 9000

Pomegranate

Views of Venice

Edward Lear (British, 1812–1888)
*Venetian Fantasy with Santa Maria della Salute
and the Dogana on an Island*

Watercolor and gouache over graphite
on wove paper, 11.8 x 17.7 cm
Joseph F. McCrindle Collection 2009.70.152

Views of Venice

Rudolf von Alt (Austrian, 1812–1905)
The Piazza San Marco, 1874

Watercolor over black chalk, 34.3 x 38.7 cm
Gift of Joan and David Maxwell 2003.34.1

707 782 9000   WWW.POMEGRANATE.COM

Pomegranate

Views of Venice

Francesco Guardi (Italian, 1712–1793)
View on the Cannaregio Canal, Venice, c. 1775–1780

Oil on canvas, 50 × 76.8 cm
Samuel H. Kress Collection 1939.1.113

Views of Venice

Giovanni Domenico Tiepolo (Italian, 1727–1804)
Punchinello's Farewell to Venice, 1797/1804

Pen and brown ink with brown wash over black
chalk on laid paper, 34.8 x 46.4 cm
Gift of Robert H. and Clarice Smith 1979.76.4

707 782 9000   WWW.POMEGRANATE.COM

Pomegranate

Views of Venice

John Singer Sargent (American, 1856–1925)
Gondola Moorings on the Grand Canal

Watercolor over graphite, 40.6 x 45.5 cm
Ailsa Mellon Bruce Collection 1970.17.171

707 782 9000   WWW.POMEGRANATE.COM

Pomegranate

Views of Venice

Canaletto (Italian, 1697–1768)
The Square of Saint Mark's, Venice, 1742/1744

Oil on canvas, 114.6 x 153 cm
Gift of Mrs. Barbara Hutton 1945.15.3

Pomegranate   707 782 9000   WWW.POMEGRANATE.COM

Views of Venice

Ludwig Johann Passini (German, 1832–1903)
Monks Buying Fish before the Portal of the
Madonna della Misericordia, 1855

Watercolor and gouache with gum arabic
over graphite on wove paper, 46.2 x 32.9 cm
Alexander M. and Judith W. Laughlin Fund 2005.148.1

707 782 9000   WWW.POMEGRANATE.COM

Pomegranate

Views of Venice

Joseph Mallord William Turner (British, 1775–1851)
The Dogana and Santa Maria della Salute, Venice, 1843

Oil on canvas, 62 x 93 cm
Given in memory of Governor Alvan T. Fuller
by The Fuller Foundation, Inc. 1961.2.3

707 782 9000   WWW.POMEGRANATE.COM

Pomegranate

Views of Venice

Canaletto (Italian, 1697–1768)
A Venetian Courtyard, in the Procuratie Nuove, c. 1760

Pen and brown ink with gray wash on laid paper, 46 x 34 cm
Gift of Robert H. and Clarice Smith, in Honor of the
50th Anniversary of the National Gallery of Art 1990.21.1

Views of Venice

Jules-Romain Joyant (French, 1803–1854)
The Church of Santo Trovaso, Venice, c. 1830

Oil on paper on canvas, 15.5 x 23.5 cm
Gift of Frank Anderson Trapp 2004.166.24

Views of Venice

Joseph Mallord William Turner (British, 1775–1851)
Venice: The Dogana and San Giorgio Maggiore, 1834

Oil on canvas, 91.5 x 122 cm
Widener Collection 1942.9.85

707 782 9000   WWW.POMEGRANATE.COM

Pomegranate

Views of Venice

Francesco Guardi (Italian, 1712–1793)
*Temporary Tribune in the Campo San Zanipolo,
Venice*, 1782 or after

Oil on canvas, 37.5 x 31.5 cm
Samuel H. Kress Collection 1939.1.129

Views of Venice

Richard Parkes Bonington (British, 1802–1828)
The Grand Canal, 1826/1827

Oil on canvas, 26 x 34.7 cm
Gift of Victoria and Roger Sant 2001.87.1

Pomegranate

707 782 9000 WWW.POMEGRANATE.COM

Views of Venice

James McBey (Scottish, 1883–1959)
Palazzo dei Cammerlenghi, 1925

Etching, 32.9 x 21.2 cm
Rosenwald Collection 1943.3.6055

Views of Venice

Jules-Romain Joyant (French, 1803–1854)
The Scuola di San Marco, Venice, c. 1830

Oil on paper on canvas, 15.5 × 23.5 cm
Gift of Frank Anderson Trapp 2004.166.25

707 782 9000   WWW.POMEGRANATE.COM

Pomegranate

Views of Venice

Joseph Mallord William Turner (British, 1775–1851)
Approach to Venice, 1844

Oil on canvas, 62 x 94 cm
Andrew W. Mellon Collection 1937.1.110

707 782 9000   WWW.POMEGRANATE.COM

Pomegranate

Views of Venice

Claude Monet (French, 1840–1926)
Palazzo da Mula, Venice, 1908

Oil on canvas, 62 x 81.1 cm
Chester Dale Collection 1963.10.182

707 782 9000   WWW.POMEGRANATE.COM

Pomegranate

Views of Venice

Maurice Brazil Prendergast (American, 1858–1924)
The Piazza San Marco, 1898

Watercolor over graphite, 35.7 x 49.3 cm
Gift of Eugénie Prendergast 1984.63.1

Views of Venice

John Singer Sargent (American, 1856–1925)
A Bridge and Campanile, Venice
Watercolor over black chalk, 49.6 x 35.2 cm
Ailsa Mellon Bruce Collection 1970.17.169

707 782 9000   WWW.POMEGRANATE.COM

Pomegranate

Views of Venice

Eugene Lawrence Vail (American, 1857–1934)
The Flags, Saint Mark's, Venice–Fête Day, c. 1903

Oil on canvas, 82 × 92.6 cm
Gift of Gertrude Mauran Vail 1973.1.1

707 782 9000   WWW.POMEGRANATE.COM

Pomegranate

Views of Venice

Francesco Guardi (Italian, 1712–1793)
Grand Canal with the Rialto Bridge, Venice,
probably c. 1780

Oil on canvas, 68.5 x 91.5 cm
Widener Collection 1942.9.27

Pomegranate   707 782 9000   WWW.POMEGRANATE.COM

Views of Venice

Carl Friedrich Heinrich Werner (German, 1808–1894)
The Portal of the Madonna della Misericordia from the Canal,
1844

Pen and ink with watercolor and gouache over graphite
on wove paper, 35.1 x 23.1 cm
Alexander M. and Judith W. Laughlin Fund 2006.29.1

707 782 9000   WWW.POMEGRANATE.COM

Pomegranate